NUCLEAR CARRIERS

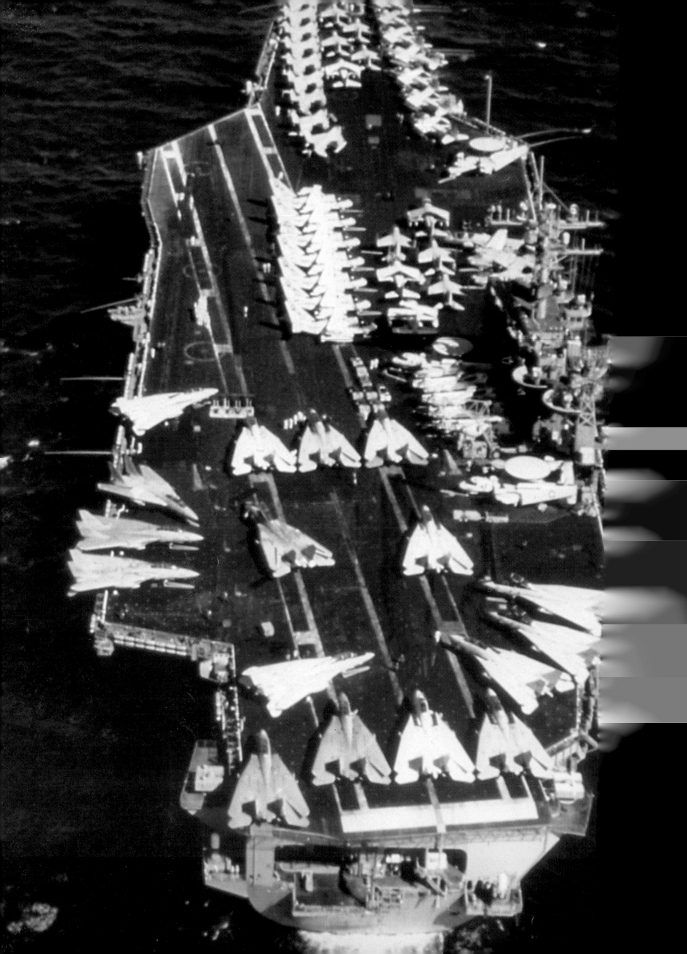

The Sea Power Library

NUCLEAR CARRIERS

by Jonathan Rawlinson

Rourke Publications, Inc.
Vero Beach, Florida 32964

The U.S. Navy carrier task force is a formidable instrument of national power, carrying U.S. influence to every corner of the globe.

Library of Congress Cataloging-in-Publication Data

Rawlinson, Jonathan, 1944-
    Carriers/by Jonathan Rawlinson.
    p. cm. — (The Sea power library)
    Includes index.
    Summary: Describes the development of nuclear carriers, the
weapons and equipment they carry, and their value as deterrents
to war.
    ISBN 0-86625-084-0
    1. Nuclear aircraft carriers — United States — Juvenile literature.
[1. Nuclear aircraft carriers. 2. Aircraft carriers.] I. Title.
II. Series.
V874.3R39   1989   88-31293
359.3'255 - dc19   CIP
                                        AC

Contents

Why Have Nuclear Carriers?

We have carriers because we need to deter unprovoked attacks on ourselves, our armed forces and our allies around the world.

A nuclear carrier is the most powerful strike vessel operated by the U.S. Navy. It is a valuable means of keeping peace and it is capable of operating for very long periods without returning to its home port. Nuclear carriers are an important part of what military planners call **deterrence.** A nuclear carrier can prevent wars from starting simply by its presence; the existence of a nuclear carrier discourages other countries that might otherwise attack.

A country achieves deterrence by having a system of powerful weapons to prevent, or deter, attack by another country. In the past, wars started because one country thought it had a chance of beating another. If a country maintains strong armed services, other countries are less likely to attack it. This is why the United States operates powerful forces on land, sea, and in the air.

Like all carriers, the object of the nuclear carrier is to serve as a floating airfield for **strike** and **attack planes.** At sea, the nuclear carrier is particularly important because it allows military activities to be carried out without basing attack planes on land. The carrier sails to the trouble spot and can send its aircraft wherever it likes without having to get the permission of nearby countries. Because it can sail several times around the world without refueling, the nuclear carrier can provide a truly global service.

Centuries ago, sailing ships spent many months, and sometimes years, at sea. Sea power was limited by the ability of the sailors to stay at sea for long periods of time. It was a tough life and hard work. When ships were fitted with engines, warships used coal-burning boilers to drive propellers, called screws. These ships were easier for sailors to operate, but they could only carry small amounts of coal. Voyages were limited to the time the engines could be kept running with coal. The ships had to come into port more frequently.

Carriers are divided into nuclear and non-nuclear, the latter being powered by conventional engines, like the USS Kitty Hawk *seen here.*

When nuclear carriers were designed, their endurance was measured not by the limited fuel supplies, but once again by the ability of their crews to remain at sea. It turned the clock back to the days of sail power, when men had to endure long voyages away from their friends and families. Yet it was a very effective way of cutting costs. Nuclear carriers have a big advantage over coal- or oil-burning ships. They can sail to the far side of the world and remain there for long periods, operating independently of other supply ships.

Nuclear carriers provide formidable sea power using fewer ships than would be necessary using conventional steam power. They are more efficient and can take on more duties because they can stay on duty for longer periods. The U.S. Navy operates a fleet of fifteen aircraft carriers, five of which are powered by nuclear reactors. Eventually, all carriers will be nuclear powered. The average life of a carrier is over 40 years. Because of this, carriers are valuable ships.

Aircraft carriers carry a formidable collection of aircraft for strike and defense. ▶

Aircraft like this A-6 Intruder are capable of carrying conventional and nuclear weapons to targets far inland.

USS Forrestal *cruises slowly on a calm sea.*

What Is A Nuclear Carrier?

A nuclear carrier is a floating airfield with almost 100 planes and more than 6,000 men. The ship itself is more than 1,000 feet long. Imagine taking an elevator to the 100th floor of a building and looking down. That is the distance between the bow and the stern of a giant nuclear-powered aircraft carrier. An average nuclear carrier has about 3,600 men to run the ship and about 2,600 men to operate the planes.

A typical carrier has 2,000 tons of weapons, called stores. These are made up of bombs, rockets, missiles, guns, and ammunition for the aircraft to carry. In addition, the carrier has 9,000 tons of aviation fuel to power the aircraft. In all, the total aviation **payload**, or cargo, of a modern nuclear carrier is almost 15,000 tons. The nuclear carrier is a high-performance strike base with its own supplies that can provide almost two weeks of concentrated air operations before they need replenishing. The carrier must also operate with many other ships and sometimes land-based aircraft for combined attack or strike missions.

The nuclear carrier is powered by nuclear reactors that can keep the carrier sailing more than twelve times around the world without calling into port. In reality, of course, the ship sails to a particular ocean and operates on a tour of duty in one area, but it has the capacity to stay at sea for very long periods. Moreover, it can operate with other ships to provide a major naval force. As part of what the navy calls a battle group, carriers can support surface and

Represented here by the USS Eisenhower, Nimitz-class nuclear carriers are capable of supporting several squadrons of aircraft.

A limitation with conventional carriers using non-nuclear propulsion systems is that they must re-fuel at sea, calling upon support ships for replenishment.

Almost 100 planes carrying bombs, rockets, and missiles are permanently afloat on each ocean-going carrier.

subsurface ships. More often, large numbers of ships are used to protect the carrier from attack both above and below the waves.

Nuclear carriers were originally intended to provide a nuclear deterrent from the sea. A nuclear deterrent is deterrence based on the threat of using nuclear weapons in the event of war. Bombers and intercontinental ballistic missiles provide a nuclear deterrent from land. The nation's military leaders wanted to provide a third deterrent force so no single

A conventional carrier, the USS Saratoga, in the Mediterranean Sea with part of the Sixth Fleet Saratoga Battle Group.

technical breakthrough by a potential enemy could threaten the concept of deterrence. For instance, if the enemy suddenly developed a very effective means of shooting down bombers before they could reach their targets, the missiles on land and at sea would still prove an effective deterrent.

When the Polaris **ballistic missile** was fitted to submarines, the seaborne nuclear deterrent went underwater, relieving the carriers of that duty. Today, the third deterrent force to missiles and bombers is the large fleet of nuclear-powered submarines each equipped with nuclear missiles.

Nuclear carriers have a wide range of guns and missiles for defense against close-in attack. To protect the ship against more distant threats, aircraft based aboard the carrier are designed to fly protective missions to knock out enemy planes and long-range **cruise missiles** launched from beyond the horizon. Helicopters search for enemy submarines, protected by surface ships and friendly submarines. Altogether, the ships, carrier, and submarines form an enormous convoy stretching over several hundred square miles of ocean.

The USS Midway was built 45 years ago during World War Two, and is one of the oldest class of aircraft carrier still in service with the U.S. Navy.

USS *Enterprise*

After the end of World War Two in 1945, the United States had many global responsibilities. The **Allied countries**, grouped to defeat Nazi Germany and the Japanese Empire, were exhausted by many years of war. The United States alone had the power and the production of military equipment to protect smaller countries. Some Allies were weakened by war, and the United States agreed to protect them against attack from unfriendly nations. This meant that the United States had to operate far from home to deter aggression.

Very long-range bombers were built in case war broke out in a far-off country. A large navy was needed to help maintain the peace. Aircraft carriers had played a vital role in the Pacific war. When Pearl Harbor was attacked without warning on December

USS Enterprise represents a class of her own; laid down in February 1958 and commissioned in November 1961, she was then the largest warship and the first nuclear aircraft carrier ever built.

7, 1941, it was a group of Japanese aircraft carriers that brought the bombers to their target. When the U.S. Navy fought back, it was the aircraft carrier that took planes to island bases across the Pacific.

A sailor loads his tray with food, deep inside the vast bulk of the carrier.

USS Enterprise *has a displacement of around 30,000 tons fully loaded and a length of almost 1,100 ft.*

The purpose of the USS Enterprise is to operate combat planes in an offensive role should the need arise.

These incidents established the importance of the aircraft carrier. Unfortunately, they were very expensive ships to operate, because they were large and used a lot of stores, supplies, and fuel. The navy, therefore, began to look for ways to reduce the cost and increase the value of the carrier. When scientists developed nuclear power plants that might be suitable for aircraft carriers, the navy eagerly pressed ahead with research.

The idea was a simple one. Instead of burning oil to create steam for driving turbines that powered the ship's screws, a nuclear reactor would provide the heat to make steam for similar turbines. In this way the giant ship would not need large amounts of fuel to keep going. Work began in 1950, and similar tests led to the development of a submarine reactor program.

A mess specialist carefully cuts pies for the hungry crew members during air operations off Libya.

First scientists had to control the heat and the radiation of a nuclear pile. Then they had to build a land-based prototype to prove it would work. Work on the first nuclear-powered submarine, the **USS** *Nautilus,* was well underway in 1954 when the navy launched its Large Ship Reactor Program.

Within two years, the land-based prototype was under construction. It consisted of two reactors and a steam-generating plant sufficient to drive one screw shaft on a full-size carrier. The first nuclear carrier would have four of these units, a total of eight reactors for the four screws. Both reactors were at full operating power by September 1959. Construction of the giant carrier to house this nuclear-power system began during February 1958. Formally designated CVAN 65, it was to take up the name of America's most famous aircraft carrier: USS *Enterprise.*

Combat planes like this A-6 Intruder are kept at constant readiness.

The steam catapult, first demonstrated in 1951, is an essential mechanism for putting heavy aircraft into the air.

In all, USS Enterprise *operates almost 100 fixed- and rotary-winged aircraft for attack and defense.*

The first *Enterprise* was a 12-gun schooner built late in the eighteenth century. In 1801 it was one of four ships that formed the first American battle squadron to cross the Atlantic Ocean. They fought the rulers of Tripoli during the war with France. The second and more famous *Enterprise* was the carrier that saw every major Pacific sea battle of World War Two except the battle for the Coral Sea. This ship was retired from duty in September 1958, just seven months after work began on her worthy successor.

The second *Enterprise* carrier was based on the design of a Forrestal-class conventional carrier. To accommodate the eight nuclear reactors, it had massive compartments for machinery below decks and adopted the now familiar angled flight deck. In fact, *Enterprise* took advantage of several inventions developed during the 1950s. Older carriers had a flight deck along the length of the ship from bow to stern following the line of the keel. If an aircraft missed the deck it would crash into the sea and get trampled under the carrier's bow.

The British experimented with angled decks during the 1950s and the advantages were immediately clear. With the flight deck skewed to one side, aircraft could be parked at the forward end on the opposite side of the ship without the fear of a collision from planes landing. If a plane missed its **arrester wire,** designed to stop it, the pilot could open the throttle and go around for another try without striking parked aircraft. In the event a plane crashed into the sea, it would be clear of the ship, and helicopters could pick up the crew.

Another British idea that the *Enterprise* adopted was the steam catapult, first demonstrated in 1951 on **HMS** *Perseus*. It was an important aid to operating heavy jets. Older planes used piston engines to drive propellers. Most attack planes weighed little more than 20,000 pounds, and their propellers had more bite on air at low speeds, helping them get airborne quickly. When jets arrived during the 1950s, their engines were more sluggish at low speeds. Moreover, they were much heavier.

When the *Enterprise* was being built, the U.S. Navy was getting ready to buy a new generation of powerful jet fighters and attack planes. Some of these planes could weigh up to 80,000 pounds and needed a lot of power to get airborne in the short space available on a ship's flight deck. Planes like the F-4 Phantom weighed around 60,000 pounds and would be called upon to fly continuously in combat conditions carrying several tons of weapons.

The steam catapult throws a powerful attack plane into the air at 170 MPH within 300 feet. To do this it takes steam directly from the ship's boilers or, in the case of the *Enterprise*, straight from the steam produced by the heat of its nuclear reactors. A special launching valve on the deck adjusts the amount of steam pressure required according to the weight of the plane as it sits ready for launch.

The steam catapult was a success, and all carriers adopted this successful method of sending heavy jets into the air. *Enterprise* had four 295-foot steam catapults, two forward and two farther back on the angled deck. With this configuration, planes can be launched from the forward catapults while others are landing on the angled flight deck. Under combat conditions, *Enterprise* can send a plane into the air every 20 seconds.

Enterprise was also fitted with four huge elevators to move the planes to and from the flight deck. The large number of aircraft carried aboard the *Enterprise* and the large volume of machinery below decks means that only half the planes can be stored in the hangars below the flight deck. The rest are up on parking areas along the deck. Two deck-edge elevators are located forward of the island on the starboard (right) side, and two are behind the island, one on each side.

Space is always at a premium on a crowded flight deck, where planes share space with trucks and tractors.

USS **Enterprise** *is equipped with four catapults, each almost 300 feet long, and carries sufficient aircraft fuel for 12 days' intensive operations.* ▶

When *Enterprise* was designed, a third major development for aircraft carriers was ushering in a new era for this class of ship. This was the mirror-landing system, also introduced by the British. In addition to the angled flight deck and the steam catapult, this aid to landing safety would be vital for operating large and heavy jets. Previously, a deck officer would wave to the approaching pilot indications as to his alignment with the flight deck. This was fine when approach speeds were low and there was time to adjust the flight path.

Landing a 20-ton jet on a carrier at speeds exceeding 100 MPH has been compared to making a controlled crash! The pilot needed more than a gesturing deck officer to get proper information in time to set the approach path correctly. The mirror-landing system consists of a series of lights shone into a mirror. This equipment is attached to the deck of the carrier. As the pilot approaches the deck, he positions his plane to get a certain pattern of lights, which indicates he is on the correct approach path. If the plane is too far to the left or right or at the wrong height to land safely, the pattern of lights will indicate the error.

◀ *Because the USS* Enterprise *is nuclear powered it avoids the time-consuming task of re-fueling while under way.*

Bottom Left
The USS Seattle *steams alongside the USS* Saratoga *during replenishment operations off the coast of Libya.*

USS Enterprise *shows off its angled flight deck and island placed well to the starboard to allow storage space on deck.* ▼

As *Enterprise* was being completed and ready for sea trials, a new generation of fighters and attack planes were being designed by aviation companies to make the most effective use of this new carrier's awesome capability. The huge pressurized water reactors saved so much space over a conventional carrier's boilers that a 50 percent increase in aviation fuel was possible. This greatly increased the number of strikes a plane could fly without the *Enterprise* having to take on additional fuel from a supply ship.

At the time, *Enterprise* was the biggest ship ever built. It had a length of 1,088 feet and a beam of 133 feet. The angled flight deck had a maximum beam of 252 feet, and the ship had a maximum **displacement** of almost 91,000 tons. The ship's complement included 180 officers, 3,139 enlisted men, and 2,300 assigned to the attack air wing. The below-deck hangars provided 216,000 square feet of space with a ceiling height of 25 feet. The eight nuclear reactors driving four steam turbines gave the *Enterprise* a top speed of 35 knots.

*The **Novorossiysk**, another Kiev-class carrier, represents the new, more potent face of Soviet naval power.*

The *Enterprise* was the first warship ever built without armament. This was a marked departure from the wartime carriers, which carried conventional guns for short-range defense. Quite simply, the navy considered guns obsolete in the missile age. Nevertheless, space was left for the later installation of surface-to-air missiles (**SAM**). *Enterprise* represented the new breed of attack carrier.

The Soviets have recently put great effort into the development of a class of large aircraft carrier represented here by the Minsk, *a Kiev-class ship.*

The Nimitz Class

Flagship of its class, the USS Nimitz *was built between 1968 and 1972 and is approximately the same size as the USS* Enterprise.

Aircraft carriers are expensive to build. Even so, the cost of the *Enterprise* had been a staggering $451 million. To satisfy its global responsibilities, the navy embarked upon a major carrier-building program in the early 1950s. The first major carrier laid down after World War Two was the USS *Forrestal*, first of a completely new oil-burning class. That carrier, built between 1952 and 1955, cost $189 million. The USS *Constellation*, one of the Kitty Hawk class built between 1957 and 1960, cost $264 million.

Because *Enterprise* cost about twice as much as a conventional oil-burning ship, plans for five more were canceled. This was not because of cost alone, however. Soon after the decision to build the *Enterprise*, progress with missiles allowed them to be placed in vertical launch tubes on submarines and fired from beneath the surface. No longer was the *Enterprise* the only seaborne nuclear deterrent. Nuclear missile-bearing submarines had a much higher level of survival, because submerged submarines would be much harder to detect and attack than a large carrier on the surface. Moreover, a ballistic missile would get through to its target, whereas carrier planes might be shot down before they could penetrate enemy airspace.

Nimitz *receives a welcome with water jets as it enters the Suez Canal.*

Third of the Nimitz class, the USS Carl Vinson is one of six carriers of its type in service or being built for duty in the Pacific Ocean, the Atlantic Ocean, or the Mediterranean Sea.

Helicopters are important for carrying supplies between ships and for rescuing airmen from the sea.

Because of this, the role of the carrier changed. It became a sort of naval policeman, showing up in times of conflict to remind potential attackers of the consequences of unprovoked attack. If fighting did break out, it could support combined operations involving other naval or airborne units. Consequently, with Polaris missiles going into submarines, the nuclear-carrier program was put on hold until the sea-based missile force had been built. Because of this, almost ten years elapsed between the order for *Enterprise* and the order for the second nuclear carrier, the USS *Nimitz*.

Construction of the *Nimitz* began in June 1968 and it was launched almost four years later, receiving its commission with the U.S. Navy in May 1975. It took seven years to get the *Nimitz* into service because a major change was made in the propulsion system. The USS *Enterprise* had not been the first nuclear-powered ship. That distinction had been claimed by the USS *Long Beach*, a guided-missile cruiser which beat the *Enterprise* into service by almost three months. What the *Enterprise* did was to prove how nuclear reactors could power an air wing of almost one hundred planes on long tours of duty far from home.

Helicopters play a vital role in carrier operations, both for supply and for anti-submarine detection.

For the *Nimitz*, engineers selected a radically different propulsion system, with the four propeller shafts driven by only two reactors instead of eight. This proved to be a better method, but the reactors had minor development problems which took time to solve. The two reactors were separated with one magazine between them and one forward. This increased the available space for an extra 50 tons of aircraft weapons and more aviation fuel. The difference enabled the *Nimitz* to support 16 continuous days of flight operations without replenishment.

The *Nimitz* was slightly larger than the *Enterprise*, having a length of 1,093 feet and a beam of 134 feet. The angled flight deck was 252 feet wide. The USS *Theodore Roosevelt*, a later ship in the same class, has an angled flight deck of 257 feet. *Nimitz* carries 155 officers, 2,981 enlisted men, and 2,800 for air operations. The ship displaces a maximum 91,000 tons. Improvements to the nuclear reactor design gave the *Nimitz* an extended operating duration of 13 years. After that, the uranium cores have to be replaced.

The Nimitz-class carriers are an improvement on the design adopted for the USS Enterprise and include changes made as a result of experience in building that carrier.

Another Nimitz-class carrier, the USS Eisenhower is ▶ presently assigned to service in the Atlantic Ocean.

To effectively protect a carrier battle group from enemy submarines, the United States Navy is developing a sophisticated family of modern torpedoes, which the battle group's surface ships can use under threat of attack.

Like sister carriers in her class, the USS Eisenhower operates a battle group accompanied by several other surface ships and submarines which, together with her aircraft, provide protection from enemy threats above, on, and below the waves.

The second of the Nimitz class, the USS *Dwight D. Eisenhower*, was ordered in 1970 and commissioned seven years later. The third, the USS *Carl Vinson*, was ordered in 1974 and commissioned in 1982. It was to have been followed by at least two more, but the costs involved made Presidents Ford and Carter oppose their construction. Whereas the *Enterprise* cost $451 million in the late 1950s, fourteen years later the *Nimitz* came out at a staggering $1,881 million — over four times as much.

When orders were once again placed for a Nimitz-class vessel, the design had to be improved slightly with special armor protection for its magazine and vital parts. Ordered in 1981, the USS *Theodore Roosevelt* entered service in 1986 and will be followed by the USS *Lincoln* in 1990 and the USS *George Washington* in 1992. Two more, as yet unnamed, carriers in the improved Nimitz class will enter service in 1995 and 1998. The *Lincoln* and the *Washington* are being paid for at the same time and that cuts costs. Nevertheless, they will come out at around $3,000 million each!

The *Enterprise* is expected to be retired around the year 2011, when it will have been in service for 50 years. The *Nimitz* will be retired in 2020. Although these carriers cost a lot of money, their cost compares favorably with other large weapon programs. For instance, each nuclear carrier today costs the equivalent of just 12 Rockwell B-1B strategic bombers and will probably see more than twice the service life.

Yet for all that, operating costs are high, and a carrier needs a lot of planes. The five nuclear carriers currently in service share duty with ten oil-burning carriers, which will probably be replaced gradually over the next century by carriers with nuclear reactors. The *Enterprise*, the *Nimitz* and the *Vinson* see duty in the Pacific, while the *Eisenhower* and the *Roosevelt* operate in the Atlantic. All can be redeployed as needs arise. All now carry defensive missile armament and sophisticated radar and electronic surveillance equipment.

An aerial port beam view of the nuclear-powered USS Carl Vinson approaching Pearl Harbor.

The Planes

Carriers exist for one purpose: to attack targets on land, in the air, at sea, or beneath the surface. They are the only weapons system serving all theaters of conflict. In World War Two a carrier would strike targets 200 to 300 miles away, and its aircraft would be away for several hours. Today, modern U.S. Navy strike planes can dash to targets more than 1,000 miles away, launch missiles against targets they cannot see, and be back aboard the carrier 50 minutes after the attack.

In World War Two a typical navy strike plane could carry 1,500 pounds of bombs to a target several hundred miles away. Now, a single carrier plane can deliver the punch equivalent to more than a million World War Two aircraft. Nuclear-powered carriers carry nuclear weapons as a matter of routine. Nothing short of an unprovoked surprise attack by an aggressor using nuclear weapons on a massive scale, however, would incur the use of nuclear weapons by U.S. naval forces.

Most duties in peace and conflict are far less dramatic than the use of such awesome weapons of mass destruction. That is why the carrier has a full complement of planes to press home a conventional attack before war escalates out of hand. The carrier also needs to be protected from air and seaborne forces determined to destroy it before it completes its mission. A considerable number of planes carried aboard a carrier are for this purpose — to protect the carrier as well as the strike force on board or in the air.

If required to act in retaliation to a hostile attack, or to defensively protect an ally, the real job of the carrier in combat is to bomb targets at sea or on land.

USS Saratoga *flight deck crew members refuel an F-14*
Tomcat during operations off Libya.

An A-6E Intruder stands ready as its crew performs a pre-flight inspection in preparation for launch during air operations in the Mediterranean.

In World War Two less than 50 percent of carriers sunk at sea were destroyed by submarines. Those submarines were noisy, easy to detect, and slow, hardly ever traveling faster than 10 knots. Today, modern submarines are quiet and can outrun the carriers, striking from a great distance and probably out of sight of the target. The carriers must carry anti-submarine planes capable of helping escort ships detect the presence of sub-surface threats.

A typical nuclear carrier of the Nimitz class would carry six Sikorsky SH-3 Sea King helicopters for anti-submarine work. Operating some distance away from the ship, each helicopter carries special equipment for picking up the sound or the emissions of a submarine deep beneath the surface. The Sea King carries two homing torpedoes that can seek out

and destroy enemy submarines or surface ships. The Sea King first flew in 1959 and joined the U.S. Navy about the time the *Enterprise* was entering service.

For more distant sub-surface targets, and for patrols over wider areas of sea, ten Lockheed SA-3 Viking patrol planes are carried. These aircraft carry sophisticated electronic equipment operating in conjunction with sound detectors placed in the water by surface ships or dropped from a special canister

The E-2C Hawkeye is used as an airborne early warning station high above the carrier battle group, informing the commander of the presence of enemy aircraft.

This EA-6B Prowler helps ensure the safety of attack planes by jamming enemy radar signals.

on board the plane. A single plane can carry up to 60 **sonobuoys**. The Viking carries torpedoes and depth bombs in a special weapons bay. The wings are equipped with pylons for missiles, additional bombs, and extra fuel tanks. The Viking can stay in the air nine hours and carries a crew of four.

Every carrier has five Grumman E-2C Hawkeye airborne early warning planes to watch for enemy intruders and coordinate air traffic control above the giant ship. Like the SH-3 helicopter, Hawkeye was introduced in the early 1960s. Its mission is represented by a large rotating dome housing a powerful radar on top of the wing. Powered by turboprop engines, the aircraft tracks up to 250 separate air and surface targets separately. It also directs the combat air patrol, or **CAP**, fighters on to their targets and helps coordinate the attack before enemy planes come within missile range of the carrier. Hawkeye can "see" aircraft 240 miles away.

One of the most important dual-role planes on the modern nuclear carrier is the F/A-18 Hornet fighter and attack bomber.

Defensive patrols are primarily the responsibility of the Grumman F-14 Tomcat, a swing-wing fighter designed in the 1960s. The Tomcat is heavy, weighing up to 74,000 pounds, and carries a crew of two. It is an exceptionally effective, high-performance weapon system capable of simultaneously tracking 24 targets. These targets can vary from a sea-hugging cruise missile moving just below the speed of sound (around 750 MPH) to a supersonic (Mach 2) bomber flying toward the carrier at 70,000 feet.

When launched on patrol, the Tomcat works with the E-2C Hawkeye to pick up targets believed to be threats to the carrier and its strike planes. Forming the combat air patrol, the Tomcats respond to warnings from the Hawkeye crew about planes or missiles rushing to attack. The Hawkeye tells the Tomcat weapons officer, who sits in the rear seat, where the targets are. This allows the fighter to lock on its Hughes radar and select certain ones to attack.

Hornets prepare for takeoff from the steam catapults that will propel them to flying speed in less than three seconds.

The Tomcat carries a variety of weapons. In the air attack role it can carry up to six Hughes AIM-54 Phoenix missiles. The powerful radar mounted in the nose of the Tomcat can track targets up to 150 miles away, and the Phoenix can be launched when the target is more than 100 miles distant. This powerful combination gives the F-14 a formidable defensive capability. About 20 Tomcats are carried aboard the Nimitz class, forming a vital part of the carrier's outer defenses.

The F-14 has a top speed of more than 1,500 MPH and can operate to maximum range of 2,000 miles on strike missions or 500 miles for combat, when more fuel would be used in a shorter period. Apart from the Phoenix, the F-14 can carry a variety of **air-to-air missiles** like Sidewinder or Sparrow, and it even has a gun. There are very few situations today where fighters would be called to fire guns at each other, but it is there just in case.

One purpose of the carrier is to launch attacks on land targets and to attack enemy planes that try to stop other strike planes from the carrier. For this role about 20 McDonnell Douglas F/A-18 Hornets are carried. By clever design, the plane needs only one crew member. The second crew member has been replaced with powerful computer equipment, allowing heavier loads to be carried. Like every navy

Hornet was originally developed as a competitor to the F-16 fighter operated by the U.S. Air Force; the design was later adapted to its new role as a carrier plane.

The Hornet has proved itself adaptable, capable of attacking other aircraft, and making ground strikes on targets inland.

Strong, rugged, and able to carry both conventional and nuclear bombs, this A-7E Corsair gets ready for flight ▶ operations.

Their wings folded to make room for as many planes as there is deck space, aircraft on the USS Saratoga are positioned for storage or flight.

fighter, the Hornet has two engines. If an engine fails, it can still be a long way home.

The Hornet has been developed by McDonnell Douglas from an original design from Northrop. Then called the YF-17, it flew in competition against the General Dynamics F-16. At the time, it was competing for an air force contract but failed to be selected. Very few land-based fighter designs get to work on

carriers. The violent landings and catapult takeoffs put extra stress on airframes. While many navy planes have successfully converted to land use, it is unusual to see it happen in reverse.

The Hornet is a very flexible plane. It can be used for dogfighting, twisting and turning in close combat with other planes. It can also ride shotgun on carrier strike planes going in low and fast against land targets. In this role it fends off fighters coming up to scrap and provides an escort screen for more vulnerable planes from the carrier force. To a limited extent, the Hornet can operate as a strike plane itself and has a useful weapon load of up to 17,000 pounds of bombs, rockets, and missiles. Like the F-14, the Hornet has a single cannon.

For conventional strike missions or limited nuclear attack, each carrier has 20 Grumman A-6E/F Intruder

Four of the aircraft on the left of this picture are formidable F-14 Tomcat fleet defense fighters.

all-weather attack planes. These are tough, agile planes carrying a crew of two and a stores load of more than 18,000 pounds. Five external pylons carry a variety of weapons, including anti-ship missiles, rockets, or bombs. The Intruder can operate very well at night or in bad weather. It has a reputation for reaching difficult targets, putting its bombs accurately in position and getting out again.

Some versions of the Intruder are converted into the air-refueling role, serving as tanker planes for other Intruders or different planes from the carrier. In this way, the attack version can reach targets well beyond the range of the A-7 Corsair it replaced, while the carrier stays beyond the danger zone. Or, close inshore, the carrier can mount attacks deep inland, with Hornets swarming over the attack force flying topcover.

Sometimes the Intruders — and the Hornets that protect them — need special electronic assistance to penetrate enemy defenses or jam enemy radars. This is the job of another plane built by Grumman, the EA-6 Prowler. It looks very much like a stretched version of the Intruder. Five Prowlers are carried on each nuclear carrier as two- or four-seat electronic countermeasures aircraft.

For low-speed operations, the Tomcat sweeps its wings forward to achieve the best flying configuration.

Harsh weather and pounding waves batter a deck elevator on the USS Saratoga.

When attacks are mounted in areas heavily defended by radar-guided surface-to-air missiles, the Prowler goes in and jams the beams or lays down a false image of what is coming through. This dramatically increases the chances of survival. The Prowler has more than 30 different antennas for monitoring enemy signals, jamming, classifying the different threats, and deceiving the enemy in return.

Many people today question the wisdom of building large carriers, which seem vulnerable to attack. Yet while friendly countries have playfully managed to penetrate deep inside U.S. airspace without being seen, no one has ever succeeded in getting within 100 miles of a carrier battle group undetected. They are a unique force, and one that the United States Navy has honed to near perfection. Altogether, carriers represent a lot of real estate, but their value is many times the money they cost.

Nuclear carriers support other naval operations, and those activities sometimes involve small carriers operating attack helicopters like the AH-1 and the RH-53D.

Abbreviations

AAM	Air-to-Air Missiles
CAP	Combat Air Patrol
HMS	Her Majesty's Ship
	Designation for warships of the British Royal Navy, such as HMS *Invincible*.
SAM	Surface-to-Air Missile
USS	United States Ship
	Designation for a warship of the United States Navy such as USS *Bronstein*.

Glossary

Allied countries The group of countries that united during World War Two to defeat Germany and Japan between 1939 and 1945.

Arrester wire A wire fixed across the landing surface of an aircraft carrier a few inches above the deck so that the tail hook of a plane landing snags the wire to "arrest" it and bring it to a stop.

Attack planes Aircraft carried aboard a carrier for carrying out attacks on submarines, surface ships, or other aircraft using conventional or nuclear weapons.

Ballistic missile A missile that follows a ballistic flight profile when rocket thrust has been terminated.

Cruise missile A turbojet-powered guided missile, which normally flies at very low altitudes.

Deterrence A country achieves deterrence by having a system of powerful weapons to prevent, or deter, attack by another country.

Displacement The measure of the size of a ship, given by the amount of water it displaces. Figures given in this book are for "full-load displacement," when the ship is fully armed, equipped, and loaded for war.

Payload The total cargo carried by a carrier in addition to all the structure, personnel, and equipment necessary to operate the ship.

Sonobuoys Small cylindrical devices used to detect submerged submarines by the noise they emit.

Strike planes Aircraft carried aboard a carrier for conducting long range hits on designated surface targets or other important objectives using conventional or nuclear weapons.

Index

Page references in *italics* indicate photographs or illustrations.